THE UNIVERSE

JOHN FARNDON

BookLife

EXPLORING THE UNIVERSE

INTRODUCTION

When you look up into the dark sky at night, have you ever wondered what is out there? You may know that the Earth is part of the Solar System, but what is beyond that?

This book will take you off into the far reaches of the Universe. Find out how new planets are formed, discover how gravity works, and learn about the Big Bang that started it all and the Big Crunch that may end it all!

SPOT & COUNT!

THESE CIRCLES TO LEARN MORE ABOUT THE TRULY WEIRD AND WONDERFUL FACTS ABOUT SPACE AND THE UNIVERSE IN WHICH WE LIVE. ★

FACT FOCUS

SPACE BITS

Look out for these boxes to take a closer look at space features.

 ZOOM

Q: Why watch out for these boxes?

★ ★ ★

A: They give answers to the space questions you always wanted to ask.

 Q & A

 THIS EDITION:
2016 © BOOK LIFE
KING'S LYNN
PE30 4HG
FIRST PUBLISHED:
©ALADDIN BOOKS LTD
PO BOX 53987
LONDON SW15 2SF

ISBN: 978-1-910512-20-3

A CATALOGUE RECORD FOR THIS BOOK IS AVAILABLE FROM THE BRITISH LIBRARY.

PRINTED: MALAYSIA

DESIGNED BY:
IAN McMULLEN

EDITED BY:
GRACE JONES

THE UNIVERSE

The Universe is very, very, very big – bigger than anything you can possibly imagine. It is not just all the stars, planets and galaxies but all the empty space in-between. In fact, the Universe is everything that exists, from the tiniest bit of an atom to entire galaxies.

WHICH PLANET IS NAMED AFTER THE ROMAN GODDESS OF LOVE?

SUN

MERCURY

VENUS

EARTH

MARS

JUPITER

SATURN

URANUS

NEPTUNE

PLUTO

No-one knows just how big the Universe is, or even whether it has a definite edge. Some astronomers think it goes on forever. Others believe it is shaped like a doughnut. But with powerful telescopes scientists can see incredibly bright objects called quasars which they believe may be on the edge of the Universe. These could be as far as 12 billion trillion kilometres away.

Q&A

Q: How big is our Solar System?

★ ★ ★

A: Our Solar System is so large it would take you over 5,000 years driving in a fast car to get to Pluto, the furthest planet from Earth!

THE BIG BANG

Scientists have worked out that the Universe began with an enormous explosion. One moment there was nothing, the next, there was a tiny, unbelievably hot, dense ball containing all the matter in the Universe today. Then a moment later, the Universe existed, blasting itself into life with the biggest explosion of all time – the Big Bang.

Q: How do we know about the Big Bang?

★ ★ ★

A: Every galaxy in the Universe is zooming away from ours. This shows the Universe is expanding. By plotting back from the past, astronomers can see how it expanded. They have worked out that the Universe began about 13 billion years ago.

1

NO-ONE KNOWS QUITE WHY IT ALL STARTED. BUT SCIENTISTS THINK IT ALL BEGAN WITH A SMALL, INCREDIBLY HOT BALL. IN THE FIRST SPLIT SECOND, THIS GREW TO THE SIZE OF A FOOTBALL AND THEN COOLED DOWN RAPIDLY.

2

GRAVITY BEHAVED VERY STRANGELY. INSTEAD OF PULLING THINGS TOGETHER, IT BLEW THEM APART, AND THE UNIVERSE EXPANDED AT TERRIFIC SPEED. IN A SPLIT SECOND, IT GREW BIGGER THAN A GALAXY.

5
GASES CLUMPED TOGETHER INTO CLOUDS. AFTER SEVERAL HUNDRED MILLION YEARS, THESE CLOUDS BEGAN TO FORM STARS AND GALAXIES. THESE GALAXIES MERGED INTO CLUSTERS AND SUPERCLUSTERS, AND MUCH LATER THE SUN AND SOLAR SYSTEM WERE FORMED. THE UNIVERSE IS STILL EXPANDING AND NEW PLANETS AND STARS ARE STILL BEING FORMED.

4
AFTER ABOUT 3 MINUTES, GRAVITY BEGAN TO BEHAVE AS IT DOES NOW, DRAWING THINGS TOGETHER. PARTICLES JOINED TO MAKE ATOMS, AND ATOMS, JOINED TO MAKE GASES, SUCH AS HYDROGEN AND HELIUM.

3
AS THE UNIVERSE EXPANDED IT COOLED AND TINY PARTICLES OF ENERGY AND MATTER BEGAN TO APPEAR.

GRAVITY

Every bit of matter in the Universe is pulled towards every other bit by an invisible force called gravity. It is what keeps you on the ground and holds the Solar System and the whole Universe together.

GRAVITY IS A MUTUAL ATTRACTION BETWEEN EVERY BIT OF MATTER. A SKYDIVER HAS A GRAVITY THAT PULLS, AND HE FALLS BECAUSE HE AND THE EARTH PULL EACH OTHER TOGETHER.

BUT HE FALLS TO THE EARTH RATHER THAN EARTH FALLING TO HIM BECAUSE THE EARTH IS SO MUCH HEAVIER AND PULLS SO STRONGLY.

Q&A

Q: How is gravity used to guess the size of stars?

★ ★ ★

A: The pull of gravity between two things like planets or stars depends on their mass and how far apart they are. Astronomers can often tell how big a star is from how strongly its gravity appears to pull on nearby stars or planets.

Jupiter is huge and is, in some ways, more like a star than a planet. Made mostly of hydrogen and helium, like the Sun, its strong gravity squeezes these gases until they are hot.

8

THE SUN'S GRAVITY KEEPS EARTH IN ORBIT AROUND IT.

EARTH'S GRAVITY PULLS THINGS TO THE GROUND — UNLESS, LIKE ROCKETS, THEY USE POWERFUL ENGINES TO PUSH IN THE OPPOSITE DIRECTION. GRAVITY ALSO PULLS THE MOON INTO ORBIT AROUND THE EARTH.

SATELLITE ROCKET

JET

MOON'S ORBIT

SATELLITE'S ORBIT

EARTH'S ORBIT

EXPLORING ROCKET

9

STARS

Stars are the basic units of the Universe. There are nine planets in our Solar System that orbit our star, the Sun. However astronomers have found at least 50 other planets in the Universe that circle other stars.

Distant stars may have planets circling them which are too small to see, even with a powerful telescope. But as a planet circles a star, its gravity, or other planets, pull the star slightly closer or farther away from it. Astronomers notice that the star's light turns a little redder when the planet is pulling the star away from Earth. It turns bluer when the planet pulls the star towards Earth.

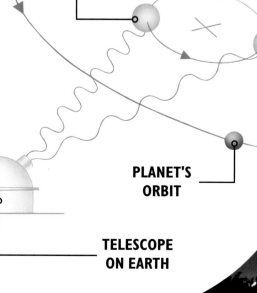

STAR

PLANET'S ORBIT

TELESCOPE ON EARTH

FACT FOCUS

THERE IS A PLANET CIRCLING THE DISTANT STAR 51 PEGASI. TEMPERATURES THERE ARE PROBABLY A SCORCHING 1,300°C, AND A YEAR LASTS JUST 4 DAYS.

Originally Pluto – discovered in 1930 – was classified as the ninth planet in the Solar System. In 2006 it was reclassified as a 'dwarf planet' – a planet that has a lower mass than others within its orbit. There are now only eight recognised planets in the Solar System.

Astronomers think planets form from vast discs of gas and dust that spin around certain stars (1). Gravity makes the discs clump together in places to form new planets (2).

ZOOM

NEW WORLDS

Even when they cannot see a new planet directly, astronomers may see a disc of matter around a star in which new planets are forming.

THE GROWING

The Universe is incredibly big, and it is getting bigger! We know this because every star we can see is rushing away from us.

The further away a star is, the faster it is whizzing away.

Astronomers can tell from a star's colour how fast it is moving. As it zooms away, the light waves get stretched out behind it. Stretched light waves look redder. The faster it is moving the more the waves are stretched and the redder it looks.

UNIVERSE

IF YOU CO
DRIVE A C
IN SPACE,
WOULD TA
50 YEAR
TO DRIVE
VENUS!

To see why galaxies move further apart as the Universe expands, try this with a balloon. Stick paper stars on a partly inflated balloon to represent the galaxies. Then blow up the balloon more. You can see the stars (galaxies) moving further apart as the balloon gets bigge;

FACT FOCUS

THE NEAREST STAR, ALPHA CENTAURI, IS 4.2 LIGHT YEARS AWAY FROM EARTH. THIS MEANS THAT LIGHT WOULD TAKE 4.2 YEARS TO TRAVEL FROM THIS STAR TO EARTH.

LIGHT & RADIATION

All the time – every second of the day and night – the stars are beaming energy called radiation at us here on Earth. Some of this radiation, called visible light, is the light we can see. Most radiation, though, is invisible, coming in waves that our eyes cannot detect.

ZOOM

HOW LIGHT TRAVELS

We know that light and other kinds of radiation travel in a straight line, faster than anything else in the Universe. But scientists did not know whether light moved like waves in the sea or like a bouncing ball. They now believe it is a combination of both – minute packets of vibrating energy called photons.

FACT FOCUS

ASTRONOMERS' TELESCOPES CAN REGISTER LIGHT SENT OUT BY DISTANT STARS BILLIONS OF YEARS AGO. THIS LIGHT CAN HELP US DISCOVER THE HISTORY OF THE UNIVERSE.

Our eyes can see only visible light. But astronomers have built special telescopes that pick up invisible radiation such as X-rays and radio waves. This means we can see much more of the stars and galaxies than our eyes alone show us. Indeed, there are stars such as Scorpius X-1 and Cygnus X-1 that are known mostly by their X-ray and radio signals.

STAR CLUSTERS

Stars are not spread evenly across space. Instead, they huddle together in clumps called clusters, attracted by their own mutual gravity. New clusters are forming all the time, but some are billions of years old.

With the Hubble Space Telescope, astronomers found that clusters contain more stars than were visible before. Hubble showed that this cluster, NGC 1850 (right), thought to contain only about 1,000 stars, actually contains at least 10,000 stars.

PLEIADES

The newest clusters are called open clusters and contain several hundred stars. The Pleiades open cluster in the constellation of Taurus is one of the few clusters in which some individual stars can be seen with the naked eye. However, it also contains hundreds too faint for you to see.

WHAT IS THE OTHER NAME FOR THE PLEIADES?

SOME STAR CLUSTERS CONTAIN A MILLION OR MORE STARS.

Around the edge of galaxies there are about 140 large, old clusters called globular clusters (right). There are often 100,000 stars in a globular cluster, and sometimes up to a million. As the galaxy spins round, so do these clusters, taking about 100 million years to go around the galaxy once.

GLOBULAR CLUSTER

GALAXIES

Just as stars are gathered in clusters, clusters of stars are clumped into vast star cities called galaxies. The biggest galaxies are incredibly large and can contain thousands of billions of stars.

ELLIPTICAL

Q: How old are galaxies?

★ ★ ★

A: Scientists cannot agree how old galaxies are. Most believe that many elliptical galaxies date back almost to the dawn of time and are at least ten billion years old!

Galaxies zoom about in all directions. Every now and then they crash into each other. Irregular galaxies like the Small Magellanic Cloud may be the debris from such a galactic pile-up.

BARRED SPIRAL

IRREGULAR

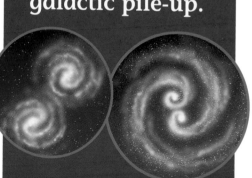

SPIRAL

18

Most galaxies are spiral in shape. A quarter of all galaxies are irregular. Some galaxies are barred spirals. The biggest galaxies are round or fried-egg-shaped elliptical galaxies.

THE LARGE AND SMALL MAGELLANIC CLOUDS AND THE ANDROMEDA GALAXY CAN BE SEEN WITH THE NAKED EYE!

THE ANDROMEDA GALAXY IS THE NEAREST TO THE MILKY WAY. IT IS STILL SO FAR AWAY THAT WITHOUT A TELESCOPE IT LOOKS JUST LIKE A FAINT BLUR.

TWO MILLION LIGHT YEARS AWAY, IT IS THE FURTHEST THING WE CAN SEE WITH THE NAKED EYE.

THE MILKY WAY

Our Sun is just one of 100 billion stars grouped together in a galaxy called the Milky Way. The Milky Way is often called the Galaxy, but is actually just one of more than 30 billion spiral galaxies in the Universe.

The Milky Way contains some of the night sky's most brilliant groups of stars, some of which are labelled here. But this is just a tiny fraction of the galaxy as a whole.

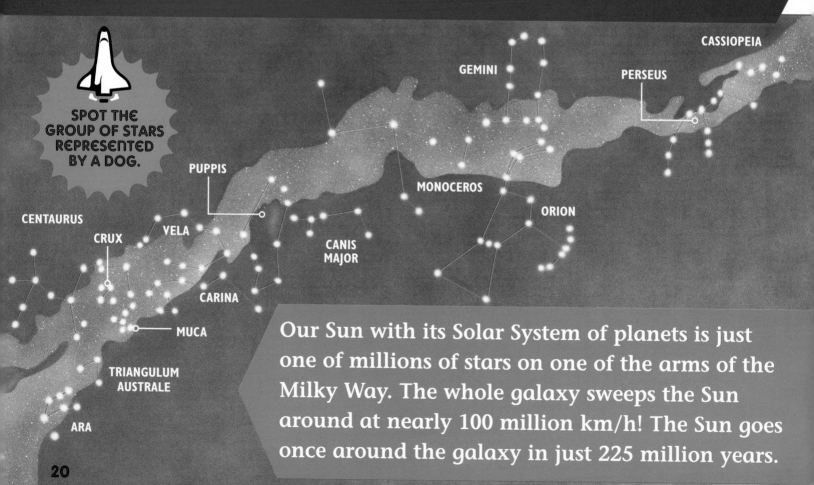

SPOT THE GROUP OF STARS REPRESENTED BY A DOG.

CASSIOPEIA

GEMINI

PERSEUS

PUPPIS

MONOCEROS

ORION

CENTAURUS

VELA

CRUX

CANIS MAJOR

CARINA

MUCA

TRIANGULUM AUSTRALE

ARA

Our Sun with its Solar System of planets is just one of millions of stars on one of the arms of the Milky Way. The whole galaxy sweeps the Sun around at nearly 100 million km/h! The Sun goes once around the galaxy in just 225 million years.

SCIENTISTS THINK THERE IS A HUGE BLACK HOLE IN THE MIDDLE OF THE MILKY WAY.

Q&A

Q: Why is it called the Milky Way?

★ ★ ★

A: If you're far from a town or city on a dark, clear night, you can see a hazy band of light stretching across the sky. You are actually seeing an edge-on view of the Milky Way galaxy with its countless stars. People long ago called it the Milky Way because it looked like someone had spilt milk across the sky.

BLACK HOLES

Black holes are points in space where gravity is so strong that it sucks in everything. These points even suck in light so they can't be seen. This is why they are called 'black' holes.

This picture shows a black hole as a funnel because matter, radiation and even space and time are sucked into a black hole like water down a plughole. In fact, a black hole is small and round, and its surface is called an event horizon. If you go beyond the event horizon, you go out of space and time into nothingness.

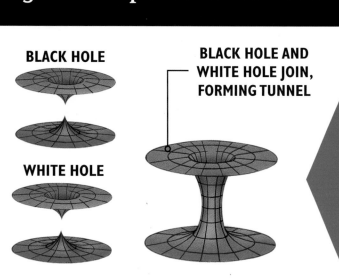

BLACK HOLE

WHITE HOLE

BLACK HOLE AND WHITE HOLE JOIN, FORMING TUNNEL

BLACK HOLE AND WHITE HOLE SEPARATE

Some scientists think there are white holes too. If black holes are like plugholes sucking in everything, then white holes are fountains, where it all gushes out again. If we could join a black hole to a white hole, perhaps we could create a tunnel, a short cut, through space.

SATURN IS SO LIGHT THAT IT WOULD FLOAT IN A GIANT BATH OF WATER.

IF YOU FELL INTO A BLACK HOLE, YOU WOULD BE STRETCHED OUT THINNER THAN SPAGHETTI BY ITS UNIMAGINABLY POWERFUL GRAVITY.

A COMPUTER-GENERATED IMPRESSION OF A BLACK HOLE.

ENORMOUS BLACK HOLES MAY BE AT THE HEART OF EVERY GALAXY, INCLUDING THE MILKY WAY. THESE BLACK HOLES MAY CONTAIN AS MUCH MATTER AS MILLIONS OF SUNS, IN A SPACE NO BIGGER THAN THE SOLAR SYSTEM.

SOME BLACK HOLES PROBABLY FORM WHEN A HUGE STAR BURNS OUT. IT IS SQUEEZED SO TIGHTLY BY ITS OWN GRAVITY THAT ALL OF ITS MATTER IS CRUSHED INTO A TINY POINT BEFORE IT VANISHES COMPLETELY.

No-one has spotted a black hole for sure. But astronomers are pretty confident there are black holes linked to at least seven double stars. The most likely candidate for a black hole is the double star V404 Cygni.

ACTIVE GALAXIES

We see many galaxies because they beam out visible light. But there are some that beam out powerful surges of X-rays, radio waves and other invisible forms of radiation. Astronomers call these galaxies active galaxies.

When astronomers look at the galaxy Centaurus-A using X-rays, they see a band of bright spots on either side of the galaxy's core. They believe these bright spots are gas particles, shot out of the core of a black hole, surging through the galaxy's magnetic field.

A photo of the galaxy Centaurus-A (left) shows a different view from the X-ray photo (above). The galaxy's core is believed to be a massive disc of gas spinning around a huge black hole.

AN ACTIVE GALAXY BEAMS OUT AWESOME AMOUNTS OF ENERGY. ASTRONOMERS THINK THE SOURCE OF ALL THIS POWER IS A MASSIVE BLACK HOLE THAT SUCKS IN ENTIRE STARS. AS THE BLACK HOLE SHREDS A STAR, IT SPEWS OUT JETS OF GAS WHICH GENERATE X-RAYS AND RADIO WAVES.

The jets sent out by the black hole at the core of the Centaurus-A galaxy generate X-rays and radio waves. They beam out radio signals that make the most powerful radio beacon on Earth seem very weak by comparison. The gas jets are 100 times larger than our entire galaxy.

SUPERSTRUCTURES

Just as clusters of stars form galaxies, galaxies group to form even larger structures. Our Milky Way galaxy is over 100,000 light years across, but it is just part of a group of 40 galaxies called the Local Group.

LOCAL GROUP

MILKY WAY

SUPERCLUSTERS ARE GROUPED IN LOOPS AND SUPERWALLS, SEPARATED BY VOIDS 400 MILLION LIGHT YEARS ACROSS.

SUPERCLUSTERS

CLUSTER OF GALAXIES

GREAT WALL GALAXIES

ZOOM

GREAT WALL

Neptune has raging storms and clouds on its surface that come and go over the years, probably driven by Neptune's internal heat. It also has a small white cloud of methane ice crystals that zips round the planet once every 16 hours and so is now known as the Scooter.

Just as galaxies form the Local Group, so the Local Group is clumped with other groups of galaxies to form clusters of thousands of galaxies. Half a dozen or so clusters are, in turn, grouped into large superclusters 200 million light years across.

THE BIG CRUNCH

Scientists are looking into the sky for clues about the fate of the Universe. Will it go on growing forever? Will it stop growing and just stay the same size? Or will it eventually shrink again – the Big Crunch?

· · · · · · · · · · ·

THE BIG BANG

Q&A

Q: What is the Big Crunch?

★ ★ ★

A: If there is a lot of invisible matter in the Universe, its gravity will pull the Universe back together again. The Universe will start to shrink, until it all ends up the size of a marble.

FACT FOCUS

CURRENT THEORIES SUGGEST OUR UNIVERSE MAY BE JUST ONE OF MANY IN EXISTENCE. LOTS OF UNIVERSES MAY BE BUBBLING UP ALL THE TIME BEYOND SPACE AND TIME.

1 CONTINUAL EXPANSION

2 UNIVERSE REMAINS STEADY

3 BIG CRUNCH

The fate of the Universe probably depends on how much invisible matter there is to hold it together. If there is too little, the Universe will go on getting gradually bigger (1), if there is more, it will remain steady (2), if there is more still, it will all end in the Big Crunch (3).

UNIVERSE FACTS

The Universe is enormous and it can be difficult to understand its size. Below is a chart that will give you some idea of the proportions of the Universe!

MILKY WAY
100,000 LIGHT YEARS ACROSS

OUR SOLAR SYSTEM
13 LIGHT HOURS ACROSS

ANDROMEDA
OUR NEAREST GALAXY, 2 MILLION LIGHT YEARS FROM EARTH

SUN
OUR STAR, 8 LIGHT MINUTES FROM EARTH

MOON
1 LIGHT SECOND FROM EARTH

EARTH

ALPHA CENTAURI
OUR NEAREST STAR SYSTEM, 4.2 LIGHT YEARS FROM EARTH

PLUTO
THE FURTHEST PLANET, 5.5 LIGHT HOURS FROM EARTH

GLOSSARY

ACTIVE GALAXY
A GALAXY THAT EMITS HUGE AMOUNTS OF RADIATION INCLUDING RADIO WAVES AND X-RAYS. ASTRONOMERS BELIEVE THAT ACTIVE GALAXIES HAVE A BLACK HOLE AT THEIR CENTRE.

BIG BANG
A HUGE EXPLOSION ABOUT 13 BILLION YEARS AGO THAT MANY ASTRONOMERS BELIEVE STARTED THE UNIVERSE.

BIG CRUNCH
A POSSIBLE END TO THE UNIVERSE. THIS COULD OCCUR IF ALL THE MATTER IN THE UNIVERSE IS PULLED TOGETHER BY GRAVITY, ENDING IN A BIG CRUNCH.

BLACK HOLE
THE REMAINS OF A HUGE STAR THAT HAS EXPLODED AND COLLAPSED IN ON ITSELF. THE GRAVITY IS SO STRONG THAT NOT EVEN LIGHT CAN ESCAPE.

CONSTELLATION
A GROUP OF STARS IN THE NIGHT SKY. ASTRONOMERS RECOGNISE 88 OF THEM.

GALAXY
AN ENORMOUS CLUSTER OF STARS. EACH GALAXY CAN CONTAIN MANY BILLIONS OF STARS. GALAXIES CAN BE SPIRAL, BARRED SPIRAL, ELLIPTICAL OR IRREGULAR. OUR GALAXY IS THE MILKY WAY.

GRAVITY
A FORCE THAT ATTRACTS EVERY OBJECT IN THE UNIVERSE TO EVERY OTHER OBJECT. THE SOLAR SYSTEM IS HELD TOGETHER MAINLY BY THE SUN'S GRAVITATIONAL PULL.

LIGHT YEAR
A UNIT USED TO MEASURE DISTANCE IN SPACE. IT IS THE DISTANCE LIGHT TRAVELS IN ONE YEAR, THAT IS ABOUT 9.6 MILLION MILLION KILOMETRES.

MATTER
ANY MATERIAL THAT EXISTS AND TAKES UP SPACE.

PHOTON
A TINY PACKET OF VIBRATING ENERGY.

QUASAR
AN OBJECT IN SPACE THAT EMITS AN ENORMOUS AMOUNT OF ENERGY. QUASARS ARE THOUGHT TO BE AT THE CENTRE OF VERY DISTANT GALAXIES.

RADIATION
ENERGY THAT CAN BE VISIBLE LIGHT, OR WAVES THAT OUR EYES CANNOT SEE, SUCH AS X-RAYS OR RADIO WAVES.

SOLAR SYSTEM
THE GROUP OF MAJOR PLANETS, INCLUDING EARTH, AND MINOR PLANETS THAT ORBIT THE SUN.

UNIVERSE
EVERYTHING THAT EXISTS, FROM THE TINIEST ATOMS TO ENTIRE GALAXIES AND BEYOND.

VOID
AN EMPTY SPACE OR AREA.

INDEX

PICTURE CREDITS

ABBREVIATIONS: T-TOP, M-MIDDLE, B-BOTTOM, R-RIGHT, L-LEFT

ALL PHOTOGRAPHS SUPPLIED BY SHUTTERSTOCK EXCEPT FOR 15TR, 17TR — ROSS RESSMEYER/CORBIS. 16 – STSCL/ GALAXY PICTURE LIBRARY. 24 – DR. ERIC FEIGELSON / SCIENCE PHOTO LIBRARY.

FRONT COVER, 1 — SERGEY NIVENS. 2-3 — VADIM SADOVSKI. 4-5 — ORLA. 6-7 — MARIA STAROVOYTOVA. 8ML — 2HAPPY. 9CM, 30BR — LEONELLO CALVETTI. 9BR — FER GREGORY. 9TL — NIKONAFT. 11TR — MCCARTHY'S PHOTOWORKS. 10-11 — ALEXUSSK. 12-13 — ORLA. 14-15 — NORPH. 19 — VIKTAR MALYSHCHYTS. 21 — SOLARSEVEN. 23 — FONGFONG. 25 — VLADIMIR ARNDT. 30 — SOLARSEVEN.